A Beginner's Blueprint for Building Profitable Side Incomes

Strategies for Successful Side Hustles

BY

EMMELINE WOODROSE

COPYRIGHT & PERMISSIONS

All rights reserved. No part of this book may be reproduced, stored in a retrieval system, or transmitted in any form or by any means, electronic, mechanical, photocopying, recording, or otherwise without the prior written permission of the author and publisher.

The moral rights of the author have been asserted.

TABLE CONTENT

INTRODUCTION

CHAPTER ONE: 1

Identifying Your Strengths and Passions 1.1
- The Importance of Self-Discovery 1.2
- Conducting a Personal Strengths Assessment 1.3
- Tapping into Your Passions 1.4
- Merging Strengths and Passions for Maximum Impact

CHAPTER TWO: 2

Uncovering Profitable Opportunities 2.2
- Understanding the Importance of Market Research 2.3
- Conducting Competitive Analysis 2.4
- Identifying Target Audiences and Niches 2.5
- Validating Demand and Profitability

CHAPTER THREE: 3

Developing a Solid Business Plan 3.1
- Understanding the Value of a Well-Crafted Business Plan 3.2
- Defining Your Vision, Mission, and Goals 3.3
- Developing Your Business Model and Revenue Streams 3.4
- Creating a Comprehensive Marketing and Sales Strategy

CHAPTER FOUR: 4

Leveraging the Power of the Internet and Online Platforms 4.1
- Understanding the Importance of an

- Online Presence
- Building Your Online Brand and Presence
- Utilizing Online Marketplaces and Platforms
- Monetizing Your Online Content and Expertise

CHAPTER FIVE:

Mastering the Art of Effective Marketing and Promotion

- Understanding the Principles of Effective Marketing
- Developing a Comprehensive Marketing Plan
- Leveraging Digital Marketing Strategies
- Offline Marketing Techniques and Networking

CHAPTER SIX:

Building a Loyal Customer Base and Fostering Long-Term Relationships

- The Importance of Customer Retention and Loyalty
- Delivering Exceptional Customer Service
- Developing Customer Loyalty Programs and Incentives
- Leveraging Customer Feedback and Continuous Improvement

CHAPTER SEVEN:

Overcoming Challenges and Staying Motivated on Your Journey

- Identifying and Addressing Common Roadblocks

- Cultivating Resilience and Perseverance 7.3
- Setting Achievable Goals and Celebrating Milestones 7.4
- Seeking Support and Accountability

CHAPTER EIGHT: 8

Scaling and Diversifying Your Side Income Streams 8.1
- Identifying Growth Opportunities and Expansion Strategies 8.2
- Leveraging Automation and Outsourcing 8.3
- Reinvesting Profits for Sustainable Growth 8.4
- Maintaining a Balanced Lifestyle

CHAPTER NINE: 9

Legal and Financial Considerations for Side Income Entrepreneurs 9.1
- Understanding Legal Requirements and Regulations 9.2
- Effectively Managing Finances and Accounting 9.3
- Exploring Investment Opportunities and Retirement Planning 9.4
- Seeking Professional Advice and Support

CONCLUSION: 10

INTRODUCTION

For many people, achieving financial freedom has become a key priority in today's fast-paced and constantly changing world. With the rising cost of living and the desire for a more flexible lifestyle, having a reliable source of additional income can be a game-changer. Enter the world of side incomes, where your skills, passions, and creativity can be transformed into a profitable venture.

This comprehensive blueprint is designed to guide you through the process of building a successful side income from the ground up. Whether you're a stay-at-home parent, a student, or a professional seeking to supplement your primary income, this resource will equip you with the knowledge and strategies to turn your dreams into a tangible reality.

Within these pages, you'll discover a wealth of information, including:

- Identifying your unique talents and passions
- Conducting market research to uncover lucrative opportunities
- Developing a solid business plan and setting achievable goals
- Leveraging the power of the internet and online platforms
- Getting a solid knowledge of marketing and promotion methods

- Establishing a foundation of loyal consumers and long-term partnerships
- Overcoming usual challenges and keeping motivation while traveling
- Facing usual challenges and keeping motivation while on the move

With a combination of practical advice, real-life examples, and proven techniques, this blueprint will empower you to take control of your financial future and embark on a path towards achieving your income goals. So, get ready to unlock your full potential and join the ranks of successful side income entrepreneurs.

CHAPTER ONE

Identifying Your Strengths and Passions

The Importance of Self-Discovery

Embarking on the journey of building a profitable side income requires a deep understanding of your unique strengths, talents, and passions. This chapter will guide you through the process of self-discovery, helping you uncover the areas where you excel and the activities that ignite your enthusiasm.

Conducting a Personal Strengths Assessment

To identify your strengths, we'll explore various techniques and exercises designed to shed light on your natural abilities, acquired skills, and areas of expertise. From self-reflection exercises to personality assessments, you'll gain valuable insights into the qualities that set you apart.

Tapping into Your Passions

The motivation behind any endeavor's success is passion. In this section, we'll delve into strategies for identifying the activities, hobbies, and interests that truly captivate you. By aligning your side income with your passions, you'll not only increase your chances of success but also experience a heightened sense of fulfillment and joy.

Merging Strengths and Passions for Maximum Impact

The true power lies in the intersection of your strengths and passions. We'll explore techniques for combining these elements, creating a unique offering that resonates with your target audience and sets you apart from the competition.

CHAPTER TWO

Uncovering Profitable Opportunities

Understanding the Importance of Market Research

Successful side incomes are built on a foundation of solid market research. In this chapter, we'll explore the significance of market analysis and its role in identifying lucrative opportunities aligned with your strengths and passions.

Conducting Competitive Analysis

To gain a competitive edge, it's essential to understand the landscape in which you'll be operating. We'll guide you through the process of conducting a comprehensive competitive analysis, evaluating the strengths and weaknesses of existing players in your chosen field.

Identifying Target Audiences and Niches

One of the keys to success in any side income venture is the ability to connect with the right audience. This section will provide you with strategies for identifying and defining your target audience, as well as techniques for uncovering profitable niches within your chosen market.

Validating Demand and Profitability

Before investing significant time and resources into your side income endeavor, it's crucial to validate the demand for your offering and assess its profitability potential. We'll explore various tools and methods for gauging market interest, forecasting revenue streams, and ensuring a sustainable and profitable business model.

CHAPTER THREE

Developing a Solid Business Plan

Understanding the Value of a Well-Crafted Business Plan

A well-structured business plan serves as the roadmap for your side income journey, guiding your decisions and ensuring a cohesive and focused approach. In this chapter, we'll explore the essential components of an effective business plan and its role in setting you up for success.

Defining Your Vision, Mission, and Goals

Every successful venture starts with a clear vision and well-defined goals. We'll guide you through the process of crafting a compelling vision statement and setting realistic, achievable goals that align with your aspirations and market opportunities.

Developing Your Business Model and Revenue Streams

At the core of any profitable side income lies a solid business model and diversified revenue streams.

This section will provide you with insights into various business models, helping you identify the most suitable approach for your offering, and explore multiple revenue generation avenues.

Creating a Comprehensive Marketing and Sales Strategy

Success in the world of side incomes hinges on effective marketing and sales strategies. We'll delve into proven techniques for promoting your offerings, attracting and retaining customers, and building a loyal following through targeted marketing efforts and exceptional customer service.

CHAPTER FOUR

Making the Most of Online Platforms and the Internet

Understanding the Importance of an Online Presence

In today's digital age, having a strong online presence is crucial for the success of any side income venture. This chapter will explore the immense potential of the internet and online platforms, empowering you to reach a global audience and maximize your earning potential.

Building Your Online Brand and Presence

Your online brand is the face of your side income endeavor, representing your values, offerings, and unique selling proposition. We'll guide you through the process of creating a professional and engaging online presence, from developing a compelling website to establishing a strong social media footprint.

Utilizing Online Marketplaces and Platforms

Online marketplaces and platforms offer a vast array of opportunities to showcase your products, services, and skills to a global audience. This section will introduce you to popular platforms like Etsy, Fiverr, Upwork, and more, providing insights into leveraging these platforms for maximum exposure and revenue generation.

Monetizing Your Online Content and Expertise

If you possess valuable knowledge, expertise, or creative talents, the internet provides numerous avenues for monetization. We'll explore strategies for monetizing your content, such as blogging, vlogging, podcasting, and online course creation, enabling you to turn your passions into profitable income streams.

CHAPTER FIVE

Developing Your Marketing and Promotional Skills

Understanding the Principles of Effective Marketing

Successful marketing is an essential component of any profitable side income venture. In this chapter, we'll explore the fundamental principles of effective marketing, equipping you with the knowledge and tools to effectively promote your offerings and reach your target audience.

Developing a Comprehensive Marketing Plan

A well-crafted marketing plan serves as the blueprint for your promotional efforts, ensuring a cohesive and targeted approach. We'll guide you through the process of creating a comprehensive marketing plan that aligns with your goals, target audience, and budget.

Leveraging Digital Marketing Strategies

It's important to fully understand digital marketing in the modern era. This section will introduce you to various digital marketing strategies, including search engine optimization (SEO), pay-per-click (PPC) advertising, social media marketing, email marketing, and more, providing practical tips and best practices for maximizing your online reach and engagement.

Offline Marketing Techniques and Networking

While digital marketing is crucial, offline marketing techniques and networking should not be overlooked. We'll explore strategies for promoting your side income through traditional channels, such as local advertising, event participation, and building a strong network of connections within your industry or community.

CHAPTER SIX

Building a Loyal Customer Base and Fostering Long-Term Relationships

The Importance of Customer Retention and Loyalty

In the world of side incomes, building a loyal customer base is the key to long-term success and profitability. This chapter will delve into the significance of customer retention and loyalty, highlighting the benefits of cultivating lasting relationships with your clients and customers.

Delivering Exceptional Customer Service

Providing outstanding customer service is paramount in fostering loyalty and building a positive reputation. We'll explore various strategies and best practices for delivering exceptional customer experiences, from effective communication and problem-solving to anticipating and exceeding customer expectations.

Developing Customer Loyalty Programs and Incentives

To encourage customer retention and foster lasting relationships, implementing loyalty programs and incentives can be a powerful tool. This section will guide you through the process of creating attractive loyalty programs, reward systems, and incentives that encourage repeat business and customer advocacy.

Leveraging Customer Feedback and Continuous Improvement

Continuous improvement is essential for maintaining a competitive edge and meeting the evolving needs of your customers. We'll discuss the importance of actively seeking and incorporating customer feedback, as well as strategies for identifying areas for improvement and implementing positive changes to enhance your offerings and customer experiences.

CHAPTER SEVEN

Avoiding Barriers and Retaining Your Motivation

Identifying and Addressing Common Roadblocks

Building a successful side income is not without its challenges. In this chapter, we'll explore common roadblocks and obstacles that entrepreneurs often face, such as time management, procrastination, self-doubt, and burnout. We'll provide practical strategies for overcoming these hurdles and maintaining momentum.

Cultivating Resilience and Perseverance

Resilience and perseverance are essential qualities for any successful side income entrepreneur. This section will delve into techniques for developing a resilient mindset, bouncing back from setbacks, and maintaining unwavering determination in the face of adversity.

Setting Achievable Goals and Celebrating Milestones

To stay motivated and focused on your journey, it's essential to set achievable goals and celebrate milestones along the way. We'll guide you through the process of setting realistic, measurable goals and creating a system for tracking your progress and acknowledging your achievements, no matter how small.

Seeking Support and Accountability

Building a successful side income doesn't have to be a solo endeavor. This section will highlight the importance of seeking support and accountability from others, whether through networking groups, mentors, or online communities. By surrounding yourself with like-minded individuals, you'll gain invaluable insights, encouragement, and a sense of camaraderie that can propel you forward.

CHAPTER EIGHT

Scaling and Diversifying Your Side Income Streams

Identifying Growth Opportunities and Expansion Strategies

As your side income venture gains traction, it's essential to explore opportunities for growth and expansion. In this chapter, we'll discuss strategies for identifying potential growth avenues, such as product or service diversification, geographic expansion, or strategic partnerships.

Leveraging Automation and Outsourcing

To scale your side income effectively, it's crucial to leverage automation and outsourcing where possible. This section will provide insights into various automation tools and techniques, as well as strategies for outsourcing tasks and responsibilities to trusted professionals or services.

Reinvesting Profits for Sustainable Growth

As your side income grows, it's essential to reinvest a portion of your profits to fuel further expansion and long-term sustainability. We'll explore strategies for intelligently allocating resources, such as reinvesting in marketing, product development, or infrastructure improvements.

Maintaining a Balanced Lifestyle

While scaling and diversifying your side income streams can be exciting, it's important to maintain a healthy work-life balance. This section will offer tips and strategies for avoiding burnout, prioritizing self-care, and ensuring that your side income endeavors do not come at the expense of your overall well-being and personal relationships.

CHAPTER NINE

Legal and Financial Considerations for Side Income Entrepreneurs

Understanding Legal Requirements and Regulations

Navigating the legal landscape is crucial for any side income entrepreneur. In this chapter, we'll explore various legal considerations, such as business registration, licensing, taxation, and intellectual property protection, to ensure compliance and minimize potential legal risks.

Effectively Managing Finances and Accounting

Proper financial management is the backbone of any successful side income venture. This section will provide insights into effective bookkeeping practices, budgeting, tax planning, and financial forecasting, empowering you to maintain a solid financial foundation and make informed business decisions.

Exploring Investment Opportunities and Retirement Planning

As your side income grows, it's important to consider long-term financial planning and investment opportunities. We'll discuss strategies for leveraging your side income to build wealth, diversify your investment portfolio, and contribute to retirement savings, ensuring a secure financial future.

Seeking Professional Advice and Support

While this blueprint aims to provide comprehensive guidance, there may be instances where seeking professional advice is necessary. This section will emphasize the importance of consulting with legal and financial experts, such as lawyers, accountants, or financial advisors, to ensure compliance and make informed decisions regarding complex legal or financial matters.

CONCLUSION

Congratulations on embarking on the exciting journey of building a profitable side income! This comprehensive blueprint has equipped you with the knowledge, strategies, and tools necessary to transform your dreams into a tangible reality.

Remember, the path to success is not always linear, and there may be challenges and obstacles along the way. However, by staying focused, resilient, and committed to your goals, you can overcome any hurdles and achieve remarkable milestones.

Embrace the power of continuous learning and adaptability. The world of side incomes is ever-evolving, and staying ahead of the curve by acquiring new skills, exploring emerging trends, and adapting to changing market dynamics will be crucial for long-term success.

Most importantly, never lose sight of your passion and the reasons that inspired you to embark on this journey in the first place. Your side income should not only provide financial rewards but also a sense of fulfillment and personal growth.

As you continue to build and scale your side income streams, remember to celebrate your achievements, no matter how small. Every milestone is a testament to your hard work, dedication, and unwavering determination.

The journey is within your reach. Embrace the opportunities that lie ahead, stay true to your vision, and let this blueprint be your guide as you navigate the exciting world of side income entrepreneurship.

Success is not just a destination; it's a continuous journey of growth, learning, and pursuit of excellence. Embrace it wholeheartedly, and watch as your side income dreams transform into a thriving and profitable reality.

www.ingramcontent.com/pod-product-compliance
Lightning Source LLC
Chambersburg PA
CBHW050255230526
45470CB00005B/2279